Love
Daph & Joe.    Christmas 1991.

# ROD, POLE OR PERCH

# ROD, POLE OR PERCH

*A Field Guide to Anglers*

COLIN WILLOCK

*Illustrated by*
*THELWELL*

THE SPORTSMAN'S PRESS
*LONDON*

First published in 1958

This edition published by The Sportsman's Press in 1988



Printed in Great Britain at The Bath Press, Avon

# *Contents*

*For*
*PAUL*
*again*

# 1

## *A word about our Founder*

Almost the only positive thing that non-anglers know about angling is that Izaak Walton started it. This is also almost the only thing that anglers are positive about. What makes the whole issue even more confusing is that Izaak Walton didn't start anything except a lot of rather tortuous blather – beautifully written, of course – about cooking chevins or chavenders, and frolicking with milkmaids on the banks of the River Lea.

Try frolicking with a milkmaid today on the banks of the Lea, or anywhere else for that matter, and see where it gets you. Before you can say Charles Cotton, the club secretary will have confiscated your keep-net and the water bailiff will be endorsing your River Board licence for fishing out of season. For that matter, who short of a professional masochist would try cooking a chevin or chavender, always provided he could find one? As soon try to cook a chub.

This historical woolliness about our Founder has, alas, given rise to some rather sickening symptoms which should be more fully understood by all anglers and would-be anglers.

The most obvious is that all anglers suffer from the permanent delusion that they are shaped in the mould of the master. They see themselves as kindly, bucolic, bumbling creatures with a rare eye for a sprig of meadowsweet and a rarer ear for the grunt of a grebe. They also believe that they dispense a brand of homely philosophy as softly crisp as the curl of an autumn alder leaf, which gives you an idea of how far things have gone.

In a word, anglers are mellow, tolerant, patient,

*Try frolicking with a milkmaid today*

gentle characters. They will tell you this repeatedly, and if you press them sufficiently they will admit that they are simply following in the steps of 'Old Izaak'.

You will note that I have put the words 'Old Izaak' in quotes because this is how fishermen – some of them even call themselves Waltonians –

*They see themselves as kindly, bucolic, bumbling creatures*

speak of him. Most anglers (80% of whom wouldn't know Izaak Walton from a seventeenth-century ironmonger) refer to him as though they shared a bottle of brown ale and a bag of crisps with the old devil in the charrer on the way to the match venue at Bridgnorth last Saturday.

The water has further been clouded by the fact that Old Izaak – bless his crooked willow-wand – let slip, probably when sluicing chavender bones out of his throat with a fifth beaker of cowslip wine, the befuddled notion that all fishermen are brothers of the angle.

Nothing could be a greater distortion of the sad but unarguable truth. Pleasure fishermen are to match fishermen, and trout fishermen are to salmon fishermen, and the whole Waltonian lot of them are to each other, as worms are to perch, and as perch are to pike. No friendlier, let's face it, than that.

Let Old Izaak listen to a specimen cross-section of brothers of the angle conversing happily any summer's day on the upper Thames.

*Piscator 1:* Thee there, get thy flipping float out of my perishing swim or verily I will fetch thee a right clout about the ear 'ole with this noble luce I have just found floating belly up, poisoned no doubt by the detergent whose foam bedecks the mead like apple blossom.

*Piscator 2:* Let thee but try it. Methinks you are an idle good-for-nothing pleasure fisherman.

*Piscator 1:* Aye, and you a niggling, tiddler-snatching match angler.

*Navigator:* How now, gentle fishers. Hast caught aught, this merry morn?

A cabin cruiser carrying two blondes in linen slacks too tight for them, and with Navigator at the wheel in a polo sweater and yachting cap, swamps their lunch baskets with its wash.

Piscator 1 and Piscator 2 unite to throw clods of earth at it. This is almost the only time they can fairly be described as being brothers of anything.

Finally, before heaving *The Compleat Angler* well out into midstream, let us admit that our Founder's peaceful potterings were more practical when concerned with cooking pike rather than catching them. And, on the whole, with all that Piscator – Venator backchat, he was far more revealing about fishermen than about fish. We shall therefore begin by taking a well-thumbed leaf from his well-thumbed book. To the devil with the fish. Let's examine the fishermen.

All in all, it's something of a relief to learn that Izaak Walton, like every fishing writer that came after him, cribbed it off someone else.

What follows is all brand-new stuff.

*An idle, good-for-nothing, pleasure fisherman*

# 2

## *What's your angle?*

The first thing is to decide what kind of fisherman you mean to become. This is not, as might at first be supposed, governed by what sort of fishing you have most of available. If this were the case, there would be nothing but gudgeon fishermen.

However, as is well known, there are salmon fishermen, and trout anglers, and coarse fishermen, and simply no gudgeon fishermen at all.

The point is that even if your back garden borders the Manchester Ship Canal you don't have to fish there. Simply by buying the right sort of gear, and then using it at least once a year, probably while on holiday, you can become a specialist of practically any sort.

The casually thrown away: 'My dear chap, I'm only interested in salmon. . .' Can mean (1) that you rent a beat on the Spey; (2) that you get one afternoon on a friend's water, if you can wangle the invitation; or (3) that you buy the stuff at fifteen shillings per pound on the slab.

The next best thing you can become is a trout man, but to get the most out of this branch of the sport it is as well to make it clear that you're a dry-fly expert and only bother with chalk streams. This carries a tremendous edge and can be justified by spending a week-end at any hotel that has a rod on a suitable river. As every fish left in an hotel water after May 1st knows not only the names of the guests but the numbers of their rooms, the bag will not be large.

*Better to become thoroughly coarse*

Spending a week-end at the average chalk stream hotel in order to call yourself a thoroughbred dry-fly man might be likened to going to Brighton with a hired co-respondent to obtain evidence for a divorce. Either, as a sporting occasion, is liable to be disappointing.

Or you can be a coarse angler, which gives you nearly twenty possible species to fish for. If deciding to be coarse, better by far to become thoroughly coarse, in fact a specialist, and then fish exclusively for something impossibly difficult, like carp. No one then expects you to catch much and is terribly impressed if you do succeed in connecting occasionally.

A specialist's approach can with care be worked out for every species of coarse fish, no matter how humble. Properly managed, your selected line makes it quite clear that there is nothing, simply nothing, else worth fishing for. Here are some useful examples:

BARBEL. 'Of course, the whole art of barbel fishing was lost after Francis Francis died.' (Few people will have heard of *him.*) 'Besides, who can afford to ground-bait with a thousand lobworms these days?'

The strength of the last remark is that it suggests either that you can afford a thousand lobworms any day of the week or, better still, that you have found some secret and effective alternative method of attracting the brutes.

BREAM, BRONZE. 'Call them dirty, slimy creatures if you will, but you can't tell me that somewhere there isn't a fifteen-pounder swimming.'

Luckily, nobody can tell you this, so you're on safe ground. Moreover, you're rather suggesting that you know not only the whereabouts of a fifteen-pounder, but an eighteen- and twenty-pounder as well, and that all three are as good as in a glass case.

BREAM, SILVER. 'Has it ever occurred to you, old boy, that 4 lb. 8 oz. can't be a very hard record to beat? These odd species are rather apt to get overlooked, I feel.'

With the right intonation this will leave the men you're talking to with the feeling that he's missing something and that he ought to dash screaming down to the nearest lakeside with a tin of maggots and claim the record before you do.

CARP. 'This fellow Walker's done some of the groundwork, I admit, but there are one or two points that even he's overlooked. Have you ever thought seriously of trying flagworms?'

No one has ever thought seriously of trying flagworms, even if he knew where to find them. Besides, belittling the present record-holder is always good for a laugh.

DACE. 'The only things worth going for, old man. Why, if they only grew a bit larger they'd make a sea trout look like a British heavyweight. I *love* 'em. Naturally I only use dry Black Gnats. Tie them specially myself on 000 hooks.'

The last part stops them. You can see their minds falling apart trying to picture how a dwarf with ten fingers on each hand could tie a fly on a hook that small.

*I tie them myself on* OOO *hooks*

EEL. All you need say here is: '*Beautiful* fishing.'

The thought of an eel is so repulsive to almost every angler that no one will challenge your right to be considered a super-specialist. If a clincher is needed, you can follow up with the bit about their natural history beating that of the salmon and how the filthy brutes crawl back from Chipping Sodbury to the Sargasso Sea.

GRAYLING. 'Now the fascination for *me*,' you begin, pausing after the *me*, 'is in the way a grayling rises.' (Everybody else has long since given up in disgust trying to understand how a grayling can be so appallingly inaccurate in rising to a fly.) You continue: 'Have you ever thought what the angle of refraction must be to a fish lying at a depth of four feet or more?'

Naturally no one has, but if he had done he would have quickly come to the conclusion that it is the same as at any other depth. But by now you will have made your point.

GUDGEON. There's not much you can do here beyond: 'I *like* gudgeon. Sporting little fellows. Did you know by the way that I probably hold the record gudgeon catch for the hour straight? Five hundred and forty-nine, and every one hooked squarely in the upper lip.'

PERCH. 'Any fool can catch small perch, I agree, but tell me, old man, how many people do you know who have caught a four-pounder?'

*I like gudgeon – sporting little fellows*

The answer to this is that old man knows absolutely no one, including yourself, but he will be too cowed to point this out.

PIKE. 'Now there's a fish I call a fish. Naturally, anything up to 20 lb. is pretty much a question of luck. It's the really big stuff I've got my eye on.'

So has every other angler in the country, but few of them have made their intentions quite so plain. Naturally you may have to slip a twenty-pounder back now and again to prove your point, but few people are likely actually to witness this event.

ROACH. 'Roach really prove a man. You can keep all the stew-fed trout in the Test at Stockbridge and give me a 2-lb. roach any day.'

Since only millionaires can afford to fish for the stew-fed trout in the Test at Stockbridge you will immediately enlist hearty proletarian sympathy.

RUDD. A simple 'Have you ever stopped to examine [this is the keyword here] why the rudd record still sticks [another good word] at 4 lb. 8 oz?'

At this point your opponent realises that he has often stopped to examine and come to the quite reasonable conclusion that they're darned hard to catch over that weight. However, as the best he's ever caught was 2 lb. 3 oz. he doesn't like to say anything. You then finish him off by tapping the side of your nose and saying just four words: 'Try a bubble float.'

TENCH. 'It's my contention', you lead off, 'that the really big tench – I'm talking of stuff in the 6 lb.

and upwards class – only feed on bloodworms. You'd be surprised how long it's taken me to perfect a hook that will *hold* a bloodworm. I think we shall see some results pretty soon now.' Or, if this misses, try: 'It took me years to cotton on to the fact that needle bubbles are the key to catching big tench.'

All anglers are defeated by tench bubbles and have no idea how and why the species makes them. Insinuate that you have cracked the mystery and your reputation is made.

Surprisingly enough, variations on the same theme can even make something worthwhile of the most ridiculously small fish. Admiration can be wrung from:

'No one ever bothers with the minnow record now,' or:

'Do you know what a specimen bullhead weighs?' or even:

'You must drop round and see the big stickle-back I had set up.'

*No one ever bothers with the minnow record now*

# 3

## *A field guide to British anglers*

Excellent as these suggestions may be, they can only be properly employed once you have become some sort of specialist. The question remains, what? Since all anglers are basically true to family and sub-species the following morphological details and field notes are appended to assist newcomers in their choice.

PISCATOR SALMO. Common in areas Scotland, Wales, Ireland. Less generally distributed in the West Country and Hampshire. Hampshire varieties are noted for opulent sheen derived without doubt from rich feeding. All have same general appearance: dun or lovat bodies, ruddy thorax, wadered legs. Entirely solitary in habit, large areas of the river being commandeered and held against all comers by one specimen. Males outnumber females as in practically all other genera. Inclined to aggressive display at the waterside during which the call note 'Fly Only' is given. Mating call rarely heard and never between March 1st and October 30th.

PISCATOR SALMO SPINNENSIS. An inferior sub-race, some say. Liable to swarm on any ticket water and even on some preserved stretches. Distribution general. Some authorities are in favour of taking this species off the protected list. The general appearance is less colourful than that of *P. salmo*. Gumboots replace full wadering, while the body is covered by mackintosh rather than tweed. Characteristic waterside attitude includes uncontrolled twiddle of right hand and air of almost total boredom the while.

PISCATOR TRUTTA FLOTANS. Found almost exclusively on the chalk streams of Hampshire and Wiltshire, also Berkshire, with occasional occurrences in the West country, Wales, Scotland and Ireland. The latter specimens are thought to be mainly migrants. There is also a small Yorkshire colony. Solitary and slow of movement, maintaining a heron-like stance, sometimes for hours on end. Very rarely seen in the water. General appearance as for *P. salmo*, though slightly more extravagant. Hairy head covering frequently infested, apparently with parasites. Intolerant of other members of the *P. trutta* group to a point, in extreme cases, of arrogance. Believes all other anglers need their heads reading.

PISCATOR TRUTTA SUB AQUA. Moorland and hill branch of the above family, but rougher and readier both in appearance and tactics. Wadered as *P. salmo* and usually seen in the water. Feeds largely off sandwiches which it keeps in the bag or basket in which it also deposits its catch. Despite apparently haphazard methods, extremely skilful at catching its prey.

PISCATOR TRUTTA MIGRANS. A largely nocturnal sub-species which can often be detected by its repeated and eerie cry: *Cortup blastit cortup.*

PISCATOR ABRAMIS. Extremely common on slow-flowing rivers, canals and even lakes. Characteristic attitude: squatting. Winter appearance is bulky, three layers of down frequently being disposed beneath long black shiny mac. Feet habitually hidden by gum-boots. Summer habits largely crepuscular, nocturnal and early morning. Cry, a sort of strangled grunt or wheeze, thought to be caused by carrying excessive weights great distances. Inclined to be solitary. Facial expression often morose. Rare bursts of animation seen when hurling in ground-bait.

PISCATOR CARPIO. Once thought to be extinct as a separate race, now, thanks to encouragement by such voluntary bodies as the Carp-Catchers Watchers Club, rapidly increasing in numbers. Largely nocturnal, and decidedly eccentric. Spends, if Carp-Catchers Watchers records can be taken at their face value, ten hours in contemplation to every one actually trying to catch carp. Generally distributed, but especially in Midlands and South. The only known species that starts catching a fish by dipping a thermometer in the water. On the rare occasions that *P. carpio* lands anything he either gives it to a zoo or writes to tell other *P. carpios* how he did it. He never keeps it, which accounts for the fact that so few carp are seen in glass cases. Regards himself primarily as a scientist.

Almost all the remarks concerning *P. abramis* apply to the other cyprinoid anglers. If anything, rudd, roach, chub and tench fishers are livelier than bream catchers. Barge skippers have before now tied up for the night to bream fishermen before noticing their pardonable error.

PISCATOR LUCIUS PISCES VIVENS. The lesser and larger live-baiter are familiar sights at the winter waterside. Easily observed field marks are the blue hands, reddened proboscis, and balaclava helmet. Except when actually playing a fish the only activity to be noted is a regular bashing of arms to and fro across the chest. Can sometimes be found in dangerous proximity to a wood fire of boughs cleverly broken from the surrounding country.

*Note:* Close season dress of the salmonoid group of anglers in metropolitan areas is largely black coat, white collar, and, sometimes, striped trousers. The other varieties named are likely to be found in overalls, uniforms, comfortable slacks, and gents' suitings. This is called, in both cases, the eclipse plumage. In rural areas there is little difference between any of them at any time of the year.

*Believes other anglers need their heads reading*

# 4

## *A rod for your own back*

Sooner or later you must acquire some tackle. There are various ways of doing this, though in the last resort you may have to buy it. Before you are reduced to this extreme, some relative is bound to remember that Uncle Fred, who was looked upon as potty in his lifetime, was indeed a Great Angler. If only they could remember where poor Fred's tackle went to. There are a few nasty moments while they dicker as to whether May (who never could understand what the daft old coon saw in getting his feet wet and suspected he kept a woman in Oxford) gave it away to the junkman, or whether that sharpish nephew from South Wales didn't snap it up right after the will was read.

Throughout this conversation anybody present who can contribute his or her theory does so. The result is that you are left with a clear picture of Fred as a cross between Old Izaak and Saint Francis of Assisi, both of them having been kitted out, no expense barred, by Messrs Hardy's and Ogden Smith's in a frantic scramble for the trade.

'Fred always kept everything so beautifully,' says someone.

'All those boxes of flies.'

'Tied them himself.'

'It didn't matter how tired he was when he came in from fishing, he always hung his line over the back of the kitchen chair to dry.'

*She suspected he kept a woman in Oxford*

'Every winter he'd revarnish his rods.'

'And oil his reels.'

'How he loved it.'

'Dear Old Fred.'

'Must have had a hundred pounds' worth of stuff.'

By this time the saliva is fairly drooling down your chops. All you want to do is to get your hands on his clobber before the next train leaves from South Wales.

But you mustn't appear over-eager. 'Any idea where poor Fred's tackle is now?' you ask diffidently.

At least four opinions are immediately given. These are always the same four opinions. If it is anywhere at all, it is: (1) up in the garage roof; (2) in the cupboard in the dressing-room; (3) in a trunk in the loft; (4) in store with the rest of May's furniture.

For a start no one's going out to look in the garage at this time of night, and, besides, there's no light. As for the loft, May doesn't allow anybody up there since the gardener put his foot through the plaster while she was having a bath. So it looks like the dressing-room cupboard.

Eventually, ten minutes before your last bus leaves, you drag a reluctant and apprehensive female second cousin up to the dressing-room (there's no light there either).

You tear open the door of the cupboard, falling nearly insensible as the strong aroma of moth-killer strikes at the eyeballs. Inside the damn thing you find yourself involved in a nightmare *danse macabre* with Fred's old suits that rain powdered camphor on you like a studio snowstorm. There are, however, no gleaming, immaculate split-cane rods hanging neatly wrapped in their cases. So you fling yourself grovelling on the floor and begin to strike matches regardless of whether mothball vapour is explosive or not.

All you discover is a tin full of old rug-wool, the banjolele music for 'Abide with Me', three cases of Sheffield Plate fish slices, half a pack of Lexicon cards and a chewed catarrh pastille.

Three weeks later you get a message that May has come across Fred's tackle. She doesn't say where. But you soon find out. It was in the tool shed.

*The gardener put his foot through the plaster*

The remains of Uncle Fred's tackle, now breathlessly presented to you, are constant to all similar unearthings.

There is a thick, five-piece rod of blackened material that may be lignum vitae if it is not actually cast iron. Made up, it is eighteen feet long. Its snake rings appear to have been bound on with tarred string. It is difficult to see how Fred, who was quite a little chap, ever remained on his feet when holding this instrument. The reel to go with it was probably designed in an off-moment by a marine engineer, for it is of solid brass and weighs about 8 lb. Attached is the remains of a line of at least 50 lb. breaking strain that crumbles to dust at the touch.

May says: 'I'm so glad I kept them. Poor Fred would be delighted to know that his tackle was going to be *used.*'

On the way home you drop the lot over the canal bridge. Who knows, it may actually stun a fish as it sinks. As you walk away you can't repress a flicker of admiration for Uncle Fred. Fancy carting that lot all the way to Oxford every Saturday.

Now there is nothing for it but to seek out a tackle merchant. There are two sorts. First there are morose men who dart away like frightened roach, through canyons of stuffed fish and stacked landing-nets, and reappear minutes later with a tin full of half chrysalised maggots.

The other kind has something of the polish of a West End car salesman, and is in fact found in the West End of London, and other metropolitan centres. You feel that he is an international casting champion

*Catches more fishermen than fish*

at the very least. He'll mention casually that he is having a day on Colonel So-and-So's water next week, and breaks off serving you with three hooks to gut to take an order for six dozen straddlebugs to be specially tied to Brigadier somebody-or-other's pattern.

Either way, you're lumbered, for it is a sorry truth that most of the smaller items of fishing tackle in fishing tackle shops catch more fishermen than they do fish. A simple natural law dictates that 95·5% of the rubbish is later left in attics, old haversacks, and tackle cupboards, or given away to some mug who is just starting. Of the remaining 4·5% which sees action, all but the half per cent is left imbedded in trees and river banks.

Just the same, a start has to be made somewhere. Why not with a rod? After all, you'll need one. But not the one you're about to buy. This will inevitably form the basis of a large and constantly growing collection of useless impedimenta which will eventually force you to take a larger house.

Let us approach tackle merchant No. 1, the maggoty man.

'I'd – er – like to buy a rod.'

'Certainly. What kind of rod would you be wanting.'

'Oh, I rather thought something that would do for everything.'

'In that case, sir, I've got just the thing.'

He has, too. He has been waiting for you to come in for fifteen years. In about ten minutes you find yourself the owner of a Super Combination Rod in Marbled Whole Cane. This has four alternative tops, three middles, and two butts. By a series of permutations it can be assembled into anything from a short evil thing like a shillelagh to a seventeen-foot monster that takes three men to lift it. The Super Combination will break your heart or your arm, or both simultaneously.

Tackle dealer No. 2, the casting champion, will assume that you know it all. Don't be put off. Pretend that you do. Either way you are lost. There he is flashing his patent-leather hair at you and swishing fly-rods about like anything.

'I – er – I'd like to buy a rod.'

'Certainly, sir. Do you fish wet or dry?'

If you are as green as I think you are, this will slow you up a little but say *something*.

*He has waited for you to come in for fifteen years*

'Er, dry.' After all you've got a serviceable mackintosh.

'In that case how does this little beauty feel to you? Just test the action.'

You try to imitate the swish he was making and clear a display stand at your first cast.

While three assistants laughingly pick up the debris you cover up with: 'What's it called?'

'This, sir? The Houghton-Driffield Chalk Stream King. Feel the weight of it. Go on, sir. Feel it.'

He's playing with fire, this boy, but nevertheless you take it from him and wave it about carefully.

Again the need to say something. 'Feels rather light to me.'

That was not very clever of you. It's *meant* to be light. A suspicion darts like a furtive trout into the corner of the salesman's eye.

'Where do you usually fish, sir?'

Out it comes. 'Well, I have a day ticket generally on the Walsall Ballast and Grit Company's gravel pit at Wood Green.'

'Oh, you're a *coarse* angler, sir.'

'Yes, I suppose so.'

'In that case you'll want our Sheringham-Bickerdyke All-Rounder in steel-centred split-cane.'

You're pretty sure that you don't want it, and for the first time today you're perfectly right.

This type of tackle merchant totally misunderstands the needs of simple coarse fishermen. The Sheringham-Bickerdyke was designed by a big-game fisherman in 1911. Besides it costs 18 guineas.

*Just testing the action*

The only thing left to you is to consult a Friend Who Fishes. You should have done this in the first place. Purely as a philosophical exercise try to imagine how fishing started at all. You will fail to solve this problem, for no one can take up fishing without a Friend Who Fishes to show him how. Then how did the first chap do it? A good question, you may say, and one which I don't propose to answer. I simply leave you with that thought.

*Consult a friend who fishes*

Friends Who Fish, alas, have their disadvantages. The main one is that they have themselves already wasted a fortune on unnecessary tackle and are now going to enjoy throwing your money about for a change.

They usually begin with: 'How much are you prepared to spend?'

Almost any reply to this question will prove fatal. Perhaps the safest answer is: 'Well, at this stage I feel I only need the bare essentials.'

The bare essentials as conceived by these characters cover such points as electric gumboot driers and a set of buzzard hackles for tying a little-known sea-trout fly, exceptionally useful during early June on a small river in South Uist. Never mind, your friend and the tackle merchant are having their best day out since they got smashed up by that 30-lb. pike which everyone else swore was a log. There are fifty-three items on the list and the bill is fabulous.

About the only chance you've got before they sell you what's left of the Kennet-Avon Canal is to ask in a quivering voice for the nearest recruiting centre for the Anti-Blood Sports Society.

Disheartened beginners should take note of the following facts. The only things you need to catch fish are:

(1) A rod
(2) A line
(3) A hook
(4) A worm

A reel is something you can always get later.

# 5

## *Required reading*

At about this stage the fingerling angler buys his first fishing book, if only because he feels he must find a less expensive adviser than the friend who fixed him that tackle bill for £37 9*s*. 9*d*.

Although there have been several thousand books written about angling – the betting is that some idiot is scribbling out another one at this moment – there are only four basic types of angling book. Once you have got these you might as well pack in. They are:

1. *The Sedge is Withered*, by Julian Berners.
2. *With Paternoster and Plummet*, by 'Caddis Case'.
3. *Scientific Angling*, by Tom Hitchin.
4. *Evening Rise*, by Sir Hubert Wylye.

Berners is the Liberace of fishing writing. He uses a lot of words. The poor chap is so deep in the purple loosestrife that he can barely hear the curlew's cry for the softly sibilant sighing of the giant reed-mace. The tragedy is that he really does love the verdantly green emerald of the moistly tender willow fronds. But he tries so hard to communicate the essentially incommunicable. What is worse he very rarely catches a fish. Here is Berners on a summer bream expedition. (Oh, yes, he has a go at fishing for everything just so long as he can be by the smoothly clear stream.)

> Tom and I were up early. Tom is a great bream man, is Tom. Tom loves bream like other men

> love carp, the great golden plunging carp, and yet others of the gentle chalk streams love the cunning, brown-spotted leaping trout. Oh, yes, Tom loves his bream. . . .

This much has been established. Tom likes bream fishing.

> As I said, we were early at the entrance to the park, for bream fishers must be quickly abroad if the float is to gently tip to the tingling bite that fetches bream fishers from their beds while lesser mortals are yet asleep.

O.K., Julian and Tom, the rest of us will crawl out of the sheets in an hour or two and meet you at the lakeside.

> As we waded through the dew-scented grasses, the wood-pigeons were stirring in the high elms and I thought how good, how very good, it is to be an angler, for only anglers know the clean fresh anticipation of a morning such as this.

In actual fact, of course, night watchman, milkmen, burglars and all-night lorry drivers share many of these experiences but fortunately rarely write books about the wonder of it all.

However, we do at last reach the water, but don't think that anyone is going to wet a line for another page or two yet. Over to Berners again:

> Tom is a fenman. He comes from a race apart, a race of men and great anglers at that, made cunning and nature-wise by the winds that blow over the flat loamy soil, land cut and seamed as is a wrinkled apple by the narrow drains and leams where the big pike lurk and the mighty

*He tries so hard to communicate the essentially incommunicable*

> bream graze like herds of fat cattle. Yes, Tom is a fenman, and Tom loves bream.
>
> Oh, do say something. But all we get is . . .
>
> The softly sweet scent of the rosebay willow-herb is redolent in our nostrils as we wade, Tom and I, through the marshmallow mist. 'Ah,' says Tom, ''tis a grand morning for the bream.'

What we are all dying to know when they finally do get down to fishing is what tackle they are using, the consistency of their ground-bait, the size of hook they chose and why. But not a bit of it. The atmosphere is thick with atmosphere again.

> Tom has big hands. But his fingers caress the reel with the lovingly tender touch of a master sculptor as he casts so calmly sure into the centre of his swim.

Three hours and four thousand words later, we have dabbled with dabchick, communed with coots, digressed with a damsel fly (which sat on the tip of our float), kept company with a kingfisher (which sat on the tip of our rod), but we haven't caught a bream. That is to say Berners hasn't. He's been much too busy writing nature notes.

> Tom has a sackful.
>
> Aye, he's a great man for the bream, is Tom.

*With Paternoster and Plummet* is, if you will forgive the expression, a different kettle of fish. (Try getting a fish into a kettle. Go on. Just try it.) 'Caddis Case' is so good at catching fish that he was once mistaken for

*All-night lorry drivers share many of these experiences*

the quarry by a West Country otter hunt and only escaped by diving head first into his keep-net.

If only he would stick to writing about impaling roach on snap-tackle and luring leisurely chub with processed cheese. Unfortunately he thinks it essential to break up the technical stuff with great dollops of writing. An example coming up:

> As Old King Sol illumes the watery wastes and Jack Frost abdicates there comes the time to try conclusions with the Finny Tribe. The Redfins will be avid for the banquet the angler spreads before them. Old Esox, sharp of fang and sharper of eye, will be on the prowl, and the Sergeants, noble stripers all, will be preparing their ambuscade beside the camp-sheathing.

If he happens to be writing about game-fishing 'Caddis Case' changes his approach completely.

> As Old King Sol sinks into the West there comes the time to try conclusions with the Speckled Beauties. The Brownies will be avid for the entomological banquet the angler spreads before them. Old Salmo Salar, silver of flank and sharp of eye, may be on the prowl and the noble sea trout, etc., etc.

After this it is almost a relief to turn to *Scientific Angling* by Tom Hitchin.

*The boffin school of fishing*

Hitchin represents the boffin school of fishing, now in the ascendancy. Hitchin, bless his dear old-fashioned heart, believes that angling is an exact science. None of this chuck it in and chance it stuff for him. You've got to tap the barometer and read the thermometer, make all due allowances for geology and ecology, take the wind-speed and direction, collect bottom samples and water specimens, before deciding whether the place is worth fishing at all. After that you go away and design a rod, write a paper on Test Curves, spend at least a year circling the water in gym shoes and a camouflaged smock, and then, and only then, attack the poor unsophisticated fish.

Here is Hitchin at his bewildering but undeniably impressive best.

> The speed at which fish excreta and allied detritus is reduced to inorganic matter ultimately depends upon the *p*H value of the water. It is vital to understand this since the life-food chain subsequently depends on this factor. By *p*H is meant the concentration of hydrogen ion quite simply expressed in terms of logarithms.

Any trout angler who has the idea after reading this that catching fish is simply a question of flinging a fly at them when they are off their guard may file out quietly now. Will he please hand over his copy of *Differential Calculus* to the white-coated attendant who will also administer a mild sedative.

Sir Hubert Wylye is as refreshing as falling into a weirpool after all this $\pi r^2$ stuff. Any angler can understand Sir Hubert. For one thing he does actually get down to fishing. For another he's such a darn liar.

Here in Sir Hubert's words is the story as told in *Evening Rise* of how he caught the four-pounder under the hunt bridge.

I do believe that 'Old Piles' as we called the big bridge trout knew every member of the syndicate by name. When he fell to my old battered ginger quill that August evening I don't know who was more surprised, him or me. The doctor had been banging away at him all morning, and the Colonel, who is a a very fair caster indeed, had tried him when the pale wateries came on just before tea.

As luck would have it, I arrived on the scene when I was one short of my limit and there was only about ten minutes of daylight left.

I tried a throw over him with a little red sedge more in hope than anger, and saw him dismiss it with a contemptuous flick of his huge tail. A second later he was up with a resounding wallop. What had he taken? As darkness fell I tried everything in my fly box. He refused them all only to rise freely each time I tied on a fresh fly. It was then that I saw the ghost swift-moth float by. A second later old Piles was up again and the moth had gone. I hadn't got anything like it, so what did I do? I remembered I had a roll of white surgical gauze in my pocket. Tearing off a fragment I quickly wound it round the shank of my ginger quill. He took it at the first offer and made off downstream as if he was on fire. I nearly lost him when he tried to go through the hatch-hole but I tailed him ten minutes later – he was too big to go into my net. Four pounds seven ounces exactly.

Experienced students may, purely as an exercise, run the lie-detector over this story and produce their own true version.

Quite right, ten out of ten, that angler.

Everyone should know by now that bridge trout can only be caught on lumps of sandwich and lob-worms dangled from the parapet at dawn.

# 6

## *What knot?*

Nothing remains now but to try out your tackle and your accumulated book knowledge at the waterside. So there you stand confronted by a lot of water and one or two quite visible and complacently cruising fish. Not unnaturally you wish to begin catching them straight away. First, however, you must pass through a testing period known as tackling-up.

In essence – as 'Caddis Case' explained – this consists of fixing your rod together, attaching reel to butt, threading the line through the rod rings, and then tying on the chosen terminal tackle.

What 'Caddis Case' didn't tell you was that at the sight of those fish (there's no need to get excited – they're only bleak) you're seized by a special sort of palsy. This gives you the impression that you have an extra tip growing out of every finger, and that both hands are coated with wet fur.

Here, as distinct from the well-ordered directions of fishing writers, is what the beginner angler should really know about tackling-up.

1. Attempt to take rod from case. Cut knot caused by pulling wrong string securing flap of case. Look to see if fish are still there.

2. Stick joints of rod together in the right order. Which *is* the right order? Not the one you chose, or you wouldn't have fractured the rod tip. Take out and fit spare tip.

*Pull a yard or two of line off reel*

3. Check to see that rod rings are in line. Take rod apart and start again. Yes, that was a fish that rose. But relax, you've a long way to go yet.

4. Remove reel from case and fix to rod butt. Pull off some line. Try to think out, calmly please, how the nylon line has managed to get off the spool and wind itself in a tight oily bunch round the reel spindle. Dismantle the reel and start again.

5. Search for nuts and washers in the grass.

6. Look to see if fish are still there.

7. Pull a yard or two of line off reel and thread it through the rod rings. Discover that the filthy stuff has somehow insinuated itself down the neck of your shirt and out of your fly-buttons. Pick up reel, which has by now fallen off the rod.

8. You have the line correctly threaded. Prop rod momentarily against tree and enjoy reaffirmation of the law of gravity. You wouldn't have imagined, would you, that anything so light as nylon monofilament could actually fall back through all those damned rings?

9. Finally get the line threaded. Take no chances and lay the rod down.

10. Tread on it. Look to see if fish were scared by stream of obscenities.

11. Prepare end tackle. Let us break off at this point to consider a few simple knots.

There are only four knots that any single angler has a hope of knowing. Most anglers only know one knot despite a lot of loose talk about double-tucked blood-bights and hook-to-gut whippings. The one they can all tie is the knot they made up themselves. To say they made it up is an exaggeration. It's the knot they get every time they try the double-tucked blood-bight and all the rest of them.

Here are my own four basics, however.

*The figure-of-four knot.* This should be known as the figure-of-eight knot. Since nobody has succeeded in remembering whether the reel line should go over or under the cast loop, it only works half the time. Hence the amendment to title.

*The four-turn blood-knot.* Serious attempts should be made to learn this knot. It is ideal for joining 0·0008 monofilament to 0·0007 monofilament. So far I can only tie it myself in thickish parcel string. The knot

*Most anglers know only one knot*

is the one used by professional cast tyers who are, as might be expected, a dying race.

*The double slip-loop.* Many angling authorities maintain there is a single *non*-slip loop. Me, I prefer to face facts. Better make sure and tie the knot twice over. That way it only slips slightly.

*The underhand granny.* This dear crooked old thing does for almost everything from wrapping up the sandwiches to tying on a size 000 Tup's Indispensable in a fading light on a bumpy pitch. In the last-named conditions no other knot should be considered.

We can now continue with the tackling-up procedure.

12. Select a float that looks as if it will catch fish and slip it up the line. Not *that* way up.

13. Take a hook, a big one preferably, and tie it on with one – and I hope I don't need to tell you which one – of the knots I have described.

14. Pinch on the requisite number of shot. This is best done with pliers, but since few anglers possess pliers and many have teeth – at least in early youth – a quick nip with the molars is probably called for. In rare cases this results in the shot becoming rigidly affixed to the cast. A likely alternative is a searing pain that strikes through the upper jaw directly into the brain.

15. All is ready for the first cast. A last-minute check of the tackle reveals, however, that you have left out one of the rod rings. As you begin to tear the whole lot to pieces again you notice that the fish have disappeared. After all they've got to eat sometime.

It is now practically dark and it is starting to rain.

# 7

## *Clout not a cast*

Before you can begin to catch fish you've got to throw the assembled tackle at them. This is known as casting. For what it's worth I will give a brief description of how to cast. If your present performance fails to resemble the outline that follows, the betting is that you have nothing to worry about.

Here, first, is the simple overhead fly-cast.

The books say, 'start on a lawn'. Why anyone should start on a lawn defies explanation. Lawn is probably less like water than anything else one can imagine. Moreover it contains grass, dandelions, deck-chairs, tennis nets, and sometimes even a fast set of men's singles. These are unnatural hazards and no would-be angler should be asked to face them.

However, start on a lawn: at least you can't fall in.

Begin by pulling out twenty yards or so of line. This is cheating, but gives you a faint feeling of encouragement. To do this, drop the fly on the grass and retreat for twenty yards pulling line off the reel. You've bumped into the tennis net? Well, use your common, lower the thing first.

Now, holding the book of instructions in the left hand, raise the fly rod with the right and smartly fling the line back over your shoulder, all twenty yards of it.

At this point it will be noticed that the line has not moved and that the rod is bent nearly double. Already you catch the sound of split-cane coming apart at the seams. This is because the point of the hook is firmly imbedded in a clock-golf number that somehow got left over from last year.

Relax the tension and start again. The second cast will probably hurl the line straight up above your head. It will then fall in a heap on your hat, and serve you damn well right. What you nearly performed is a steeple cast, and please remember not to run before you can walk.

You get the line behind you at the third attempt, and are so overcome by this that you totally fail to make the reciprocal forward movement. Result: the fly lands on the rose pergola. Go next door to borrow your step-ladder so that you can get the thing down, and miss two turns.

After an hour and a half of continuous effort you do manage to make the line whistle back and forth through the air with a most satisfying swish, punctuated at every fourth cast with an equally satisfying crack. This is caused by the fly parting company with the cast. As you have chosen a yellow palmer, and it invariably falls into a bed of marigolds, this slows things up a bit. Just remember that it's all your fault: you were told to pause on the back-cast.

At about this juncture the cat enters. It is always the same cat, a large, flat-headed tabby tom with an insolent lope and a pair of ears that look as if they have been trimmed with a ticket punch.

The cat walks deliberately into the centre of the lawn just as you are putting down your fly with superb skill exactly above the nose of a 4-lb. trout lying to the right of the occasional table bearing the tea tray which your wife has just deposited.

Rising beautifully, the cat swallows the fly with the half roll of the confident taker well on the feed. Feeling the iron he makes off in a first rush that would put to shame a record sea trout. The rod bucks in your hands, and the reel begins to scream with that spine-tingling screech that every angler knows and loves. Five, ten, fifteen, twenty yards rip off the reel, but you've still got him on. Putting on all the side-strain you know how, you stop him on top of the garden fence. And then he bounds straight into, or rather through, the cold frame. You manage to recover a little line, but he's off again in one of those lightning rushes. Wind the line back on to the reel somehow. He's coming fast towards you. And then it happens. With the sure instinct of a thoroughbred fighter he's round the occasional table and up on to the coal bunker roof, leaving only the foam of a cream sponge to show where he broke you.

Never mind. You can always say that he weighed at least 10 lb.

# 8

## *The gentle art*

Fishermen should never lose sight of the fact that fish make it a lot easier for them by being very careless eaters. Among the things that fish have been known to swallow can be included: slugs, frogs, bullock's pith, greaves, valve-rubber, macaroni, large lumps of shining tin, banana cubes, parboiled potatoes, sections of old inner tube, and once, in the case of a very old tench I knew in a gravel pit at Aldermaston, two shirt-buttons and a crown-cork.

From this it can be seen that fish are not choosey. However, since most of the things mentioned above are utterly repulsive, downright unlikely, or completely unobtainable, nobody bothers much with them.

If you don't believe this, then try walking into your butcher's and ordering a pound, gallon, or however they measure the stuff, of bullock's pith. You will almost certainly be looked at askance, and may possibly be asked to take your trade elsewhere.

So you must turn to something else. Fortunately there are alternatives. If you are to fish successfully, the properties, capture, care and maintenance, and employment of these must be studied.

Take, for example, the common or garden worm. Worms can be dug up from commons or gardens, but since this raises all sorts of unnecessary issues like next spring's daffodils, the dead guinea-pig the children buried last July, and the bone your wife hoped the dog had finally lost, digging is better left alone. Only in rare cases where the vegetable patch has got to be turned over before you can go fishing next Saturday should it be attempted.

Better by far to become a worm stalker.

Worm stalkers wear plimsolls, and operate at dead of night. A torch and the natural instincts of the hunter are the only other requirements.

Worm stalkers take advantage of the little-known fact that worms are moon-bathers. As can be imagined they would much rather sun-bathe but the predatory attitude of birds has rendered the acquiring of a rich tan unthinkable.

This makes it obvious that the proverb about the early bird getting the worm is pretty average rubbish. True, an occasional early bird does get a slothful, sleepy or disoriented worm – the sort that doesn't know whether it's coming or going. But if only birds would learn to operate at night (they wouldn't even have to fly: just walking about would do) they'd trip over layabout lobworms that can be found protruding from holes in lawns and flower beds just gossiping with each other.

Some people maintain that there are few more beautiful and reassuring sights than the two ends of a lobworm courting in the evening gloaming, but worm stalkers must put such thoughts resolutely aside.

The technique of nocturnal worm capture is relatively simple. Grasping his torch, the hunter creeps about on plimsolled tiptoe until he spots a worm. About six inches of this is usually to be seen basking arrogantly on the sward. However, a prehensile seventh inch is hooked well into the worm's front door. It is on this that the stalker must focus his attention, for at the first sign of trouble the worm shoots smartly backwards like a suddenly released sock-suspender and disappears from view, pulling the hatch shut after it.

The solution is to aim at the tail end before the worm knows what's hit it and close thumb and forefinger neatly round the hole.

Many anglers have found this pastime so utterly absorbing that they have given up fishing and simply concentrated on worm catching.

As a footnote it should be added that many a dull party can be enlivened by the casual suggestion, 'Let's go out on the lawn and catch worms.' The screams of laughter as the women guests race each other for a juicy lob or find themselves left holding half a gilt-tail have to be heard to be believed.

The next step is to imbue the worms with the correct offensive spirit. After all, it's useless to expect a worm, snatched suddenly from a soft domestic background and a good home, to get in there and fight with, say, a 4-lb. chub.

All angling authorities agree that worm must be toughened. For this purpose vermiculturists construct a kind of assault course. This consists of a tin filled with moist sphagnum moss. But, since no one outside the membership of the Royal Horticultural Society knows what sphagnum is, where to find it, or even how to spell it, most worm trainees settle for grass, dead leaves and the stuffing out of a derelict bolster. Through this nauseating mixture, suitably moistened, the worms romp happily from top to bottom where they tie themselves into an inextricable and rather beastly knot. The trainer then turns the tin

*'Let's go out on the lawn and catch worms'*

the other way up and off they go again. Tired worms are revived with a sprinkling of milk and the obviously exhausted ones are returned to unit as lacking moral fibre.

Worms will keep this up endlessly, becoming tougher at every trip. A simple test reveals when they are ready for combat duty. Hold them close to a goldfish bowl. Those that lash their tails in an obviously aggressive fashion should be drafted immediately.

Though the question of how a worm becomes a worm is still something of a mystery to the layman, the life-history of that popular little creature the gentle, or maggot, may be studied and understood by any keen naturalist whose neighbours have lost their sense of smell.

If you wish to have maggots about the place, simply hang up a well-decayed sheep's head or dead rabbit. Some breeders prefer to do so outside the house, if only because the blow flies will have a better chance to reach the target. Rearing your maggots outdoors does, of course, rob the pursuit of much of its fascination. Outdoor breeders miss the endearing plop of the little pets falling steadily into the tin put to catch them.

Though maggots cannot actually be trained to throttle fish in the manner of the really aggressive lobworm they can be taught fish enticement through the use of cosmetics. Fish go particularly sloppy about blue, gold, and scarlet maggots. Making up maggots is held by some purists to be an unnatural practice, but since no one has yet been able to tell a boy from a girl maggot, it is doubtful whether any serious objection can be sustained.

Maggots have one serious drawback. At the first sign of trouble they turn into a chrysalis, when they become almost entirely useless for fishing purposes. There is only one thing worse than a maggot that has turned into a chrysalis and that is a chrysalis that has turned into a fly. Though maggots chrysalise in a particularly sly way – one moment there they are wriggling happily in the tin and the next they're giving an imitation of a miniature Havana cigar – the angler can always tell when the fly stage has been achieved. Simply hold the bait tin close to the ear, when a distinct buzzing will be heard. Make no attempt to remove the lid, but lend your bait tin to the next person who asks you. Many an angling friendship, if not angler, has been struck as the result of such a gesture.

All unsuccessful anglers suspect all successful anglers of having a secret, and therefore unfair, bait. Such a lure has been sought for in a manner which makes the quest for the Philosopher's Stone seem like a children's party treasure hunt. There is in fact one sure-fire bait over which all fish go crazy, but its processing is long and arduous.

First of all you have to grow the seeds, then crush them, purify the result, mix it with water, pound the paste thus made with several other ingredients, heat very thoroughly to exactly the right temperature and maintain this heat for precisely the correct time. The result is then removed and folded in a sterilised container.

Fortunately there is no need to go to all this trouble yourself. You can buy the stuff ready-made in the shops.

The mystery is why fish, the idiots, should go so daft over something they're never likely to meet in real life.

Tell me, how many times have you seen a sliced, wrapped loaf growing on the bed of a river?

# 9

## *How to outwit an eel*

If earlier in this book I have given the impression that some anglers become specialists deliberately, I wish now to about face and take the opposite, and real, viewpoint. If you find yourself fishing exclusively for one sort of fish, it's probably because you can't catch anything else. Take eels, for instance.

You may ask, quite understandably, who in his right mind would take an eel, and there you have the key to the whole eel situation. People do not take eels: eels take them.

As far as I have been able to make out from personal observation, eels lead a loathsome life. After that long, long swim from the Sargasso Sea that people keep telling us about, and before that long, long swim back to reproduce their beastly kind, there comes a period in fresh water which eels spend terrorising innocent fish and annoying fishermen. They do this by sleeping all day in a kind of slithy trance, only waking as the temperature falls sufficiently for it to be worth one's going fishing. They then ooze about the river bed guzzling sewage, offal, old bicycle frames and anglers' leger weights. There is nothing an eel likes more than to find a lobworm put out for bream or tench. He sucks this down with the delicacy of a dowager sipping China tea, knowing very well that this will make the angler's float tremble in a quite un-eel-like way. On the bank, the fisherman puts down his evening paper, shouts to his friend, 'the bream are coming on' and prepares to strike a six-pounder when the float finally glides away.

So, to liven things up, the eel takes the float under with a pop like a well-ejected champagne cork, and goes into his routine, which is considerable. Though it may have escaped the notice of zoologists, eels are brilliant mimics. They have the ability to imitate exactly the antics of any species of hooked fish you care to name.

'Got a big 'un here,' the lucky angler shouts.

'What is it?' calls his friend.

'Whopping great bream.'

The eel hears this. It is what he has been waiting for. He lashes his tail about and begins to jag like a perch.

The angler's companion has now come running up, having seen the bend the eel has put into the rod.

'Garn,' he says, 'that's no bream. That's a perch.'

The eel does another quick-change act, this time diving straight for the bottom.

'Ever see a perch fight like that,' screams the angler who is now close to cerebral thrombosis and sees himself receiving at least four prize rods from grateful national newspapers. 'Tell you what it is, it's a big tench.'

'More like a trout.'

'Barbel.'

'Could be a carp.'

No one thinks of saying that it is an eel. This infuriates the eel. It feels that it is now time to break out its battle ensign and proclaim its eeldom. For this purpose it has been keeping one of its beady little eyes on an abandoned perambulator well out on the bottom in mid-stream. It makes for this and wraps its tail round one of the wheels with a crack like a stockwhip.

And there it will remain, if necessary until it is time to go back to the Sargasso Sea, or the perambulator wheel come off, or the angler commits suicide, or, as is most likely, the hook straightens.

Just occasionally the eel decides to teach the angler a sharp lesson, in which case it allows itself to be landed.

Should you ever find yourself in the unfortunate position of landing an eel, resign yourself to a traumatic experience that may easily mark the mind for life.

Eels, it should be noted, like to be scooped up in landing nets. This gives them a chance to fall through the meshes so that you are forced to cut them loose. In the special panic that eels engender, you can easily, and usually do, cut the landing net and

*Who in his right mind would take an eel?*

not the trace. Should you succeed in cutting the trace, the eel rapidly returns to the water having achieved its main objects: (a) to give you a nasty turn; and (b) to spread slime all over everything. It can now go back to the South Atlantic and boast about this, and the sooner the better.

The text-books, as usual, have the answers pat. To quieten eels, the pundits say, simply give them a sharp blow on the tail, since this, perversely, is where eels keep their nerve centres. Though this may sound straightforward enough, in practice it results in a series of wild and haphazard thrashings and bangings. I have seen an angler, in an attempt to strike an eel a sharp blow on the tail, smash his wristwatch, three bottles of light ale, and the wind-screen of a nearby car.

Other authors hold that an eel can be made docile if rolled in brickdust or ashes. Few anglers, however keen, carry these commodities to the waterside in sufficient quantity to be effective. One attempt to roll an eel in anything will quickly convince the operator that he would do far better to roll himself in brickdust: he will certainly need his nerves quietened by something, and brickdust may just do the trick.

Another theory has it that an eel becomes baffled if wrapped up in newspaper, and that once dropped on an open sheet of, say, *The Times*, the animal will enshroud itself happily and settle down to enjoy the fourth leader when, reduced to a suitably somnolent state, it can be dispatched at leisure.

But the only really practical suggestion I can make to the fisherman who finds himself being played by an eel is to run, not walk, away from the water for at least one hundred yards, towing the thing behind him. He must then throw himself on the creature, showering on it brickdust, ashes and rolled newspapers, while simultaneously striking out with clubs, knives and machetes. One or all of these things may bring results, particularly if a lucky blow severs the eel's head. Headless eels have been known to expire: but only just.

The only angler I have ever seen actually dominate an eel was an aged fisherman sitting by a Belgian canal. He used clothes' line and a stout bamboo pole and was accompanied by a wall-eyed Alsatian dog. On hooking an eel – there appeared to be nothing else in the canal – he simply hurled it straight out of the water and into a thicket behind him, where the dog retrieved it.

I leave despondent eel catchers with this thought.

# 10

## *Night must fall*

Anyone who fishes exclusively for carp is almost certifiable. Those who claim only to fish for carp at night should be led quickly away to the psychiatrist's couch before they do themselves permanent injury.

Night fishers say they go night fishing because the fish are less wary, or more hungry, or both, when the sun goes down. This disguises the real truth which is simply that night fishers don't sleep well, or have quarrelled with their wives.

I once went night fishing for carp. I will now describe the experience so that it may be a lesson to us all.

To begin with I had collected all the things that night fishers say you need. These included, as far as I remember – and I don't care to think of it in too much detail – rubber cushions, a small folding deck-chair, a blanket, two vacuum flasks, not to mention a stone and a half of pulped bread, a wet sack to put the carp in (don't ask me why), and, just to make the whole thing seem more realistic, a carp rod, giant landing net and the usual bag full of rubbish that one carries to go fishing.

The whole exercise was made more complicated from the outset because, to be strictly accurate, I hadn't got permission to fish this lake. I had therefore to make a careful and circuitous approach-stalk through about a mile and a half of dense rhododendron bushes. Because I am not playing this for easy laughs I shall resist telling you what *that* was like.

At the end of this I was in such a pother that I sat down and prepared to tackle-up in front of a large ornamental rose-bed which seemed at that moment closely to resemble a small carp pond. It was only after throwing the first fistful of ground-bait and seeing its progress suddenly arrested in mid-air by a polyanthus that I realised my mistake.

On reaching the lakeside proper I quickly summed up the position. I was on a high bank about six feet above the water. Care would have to be exercised lest an unwary movement put me over the edge and into the deep end. It was something of a surprise, therefore, when some five minutes later I slid an incautious foot over the bank to find that I had got a bootful. Further reconnaissance revealed that the water was, in fact, six inches below the level of the bank.

My night fishing acquaintances had warned me that it was fatal to go around flashing bright lights (quite apart from anything else, the owner of the house might spot me). I had therefore armed myself with a pencil torch of the type carried by doctors for peering down patients' gullets and ear-holes. The torch was so designed that the switch had to be pressed continuously if it was to stay on.

I have now set the scene for you: the next bit you can fill in for yourselves.

Holding the torch in one hand and pressing the switch continuously, attempt to tie a No. 4 eyed hook to a nylon monofilament line, bearing in mind that you are standing in a thicket on the darkest night since the birth of the solar system. Just to encourage you an owl is tuning up six inches from your right ear while a bat is making low flying passes across your

*The real truth is that night fishers have quarrelled with their wives*

hair. And all this while, as your fingers attempt one of the labours that somehow got left off Hercules' list, giant carp are leaping and cavorting, swirling and splashing, and generally making a noise like sacks of cement being dumped from a helicopter five hundred feet up above a vat of treacle. It is very unnerving.

As dawn was approaching I did eventually get the hook tied on with a knot that would have made a mirror carp crack its plate-glass scales with laughing. Keen night fishers may care to note that I used seven right-handed grannies topped off with the one I keep for putting blobs of sealing wax on when doing up registered parcels.

The next revelation came at the casting stage. Now carp are creatures of gross appetite. Very young carp will eat lumps of bread the size of golf balls, but, for the senior inhabitants, nothing under tennis-ball girth will do. Never having tried baiting a hook with anything of that calibre I quickly found myself in trouble with the sheer mechanics of the problem.

I'd press this foul mass of dough on to the hook, hoist it into mid-air and begin a slow, graceful back-swing preparatory to the deft forward cast that would put the bait right into the middle of the lake. Unknown to me, all this time, the bait was taking advantage of the darkness to detach itself from the hook. The final separation always came just as I was going into the forward cast, with the result that an enormous amount of energy was expended in throwing an empty hook into the hawthorn bushes five yards to my left.

It seemed that I didn't have a big enough hook: or, alternatively, I had too big a bait. But as I had no larger hooks and the five small ones I had brought along were all lost in the hawthorn bush, there was not much to do except wait for daylight to come.

Which is where the deck-chair and blanket should have come in, but for the fact that somewhere way back in the rhododendron bushes I had dropped the blanket, probably at the precise moment I put my foot through the canvas of the deck-chair.

Thinking about it calmly I realise that I should have: (1) practised casting with a big bait in daylight at home; (2) tied my hook to the line before leaving the house; (3) taken a sensible torch.

Before I leave the subject for good and all and allow the scar-tissue to form over the incident, I have just one important piece of personal advice to pass on to would-be night fishers.

It is simply this: pull the eiderdown up snugly to the chin and turn over.

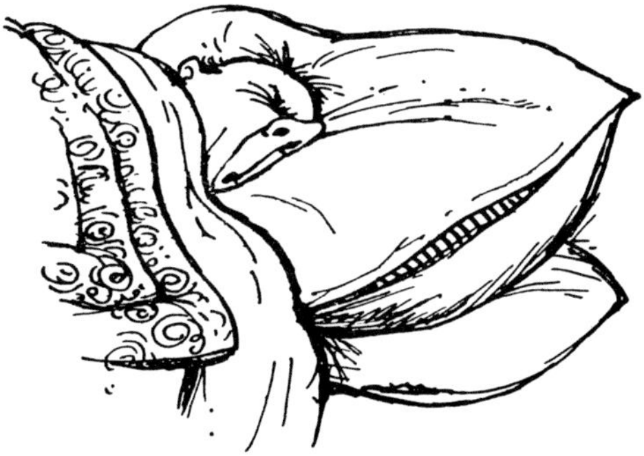

# 11

## *A likely story*

Round no creature since the brontosaurus has such a fabric of legendary rot accreted as the pike. This whole vast mythology is known to the more Waltonian among us as 'Pike Lore'. Practically every word of it is false.

It starts from the simple folk-belief that every piece of water, from the pit behind the brickworks upwards, holds, if not an actual record, then a monster. The growth of this belief, which is worth many pints when correctly handled by the local inhabitants, has been aided by the blatant opacity of the average sheet of water, still or running, in these islands. Since you can't see through the stuff, no one can prove you a liar.

A few of the waters concerned don't hold pike at all. The disturbances seen at the surface from time to time are probably caused by vast unleashings of marsh gas, or by bricks hurled at half light by those interested in perpetuating the monster. Everyone feels a lot cosier if it can be put round that the big pike is on the move again.

Most waters do harbour pike, however, and on the rare occasions when such lakes are netted or drained by some natural or artificial catastrophe the monster lies revealed. He invariably weighs exactly 8 lb.

The rot – and I do mean rot – probably started with the alleged Kenmure monster. This was supposed to have been caught in Loch Ken in seventeen-hundred-and-something by Lord Somebody's bailiff and to have weighed 72 lb. Not content with the undoubted fact that he had landed a thumping great fish (the possibility exists of course that the pike had got so big and old that it had died and was found washed up), the bailiff immediately put round the wild rumour that he had caught it on a fly. This was because he was a Scot and to fish with anything other than a fly was unthinkable.

However, if a pike that size would eat a fly, it was argued, then the species would eat anything. This was the root of the second pike myth: namely, that pike will eat anything.

Among the things which pike are said to have eaten are: dogs, pigs, swans, gold rings (inscribed with a date at least four hundred years prior to the year of discovery), gum-boots (with and without

*Pike will eat anything*

leg filling), toy yachts, live-bait floats, picnic baskets, and handbags.

The list of items they have had a go at is far more exotic. It includes human bathers, horses' snouts, donkeys' hindlegs, babies, nudists, cows' tails, sheeps' noses and a variety of bigger and less animal and human extremities.

Keen students of pike lore are sooner or later bound to run across the persistent and splendidly unauthenticated pike sub-myth that somewhere in Norfolk there exists a pub in which stands a glass case containing not only a beautifully taxidermised twenty-pounder but the exquisitely mounted fingers of the man who tried to land it.

From here we pass on naturally to pike myth number three: this is an article of faith among pike fishermen. It is that all pike eat an average of at least their own weight in a day.

This poses some pretty problems with which most of us quite rightly refuse to be concerned. Such as what happens on the days when pike don't eat at all. Anyone who has been pike fishing can confirm that these occur, and all too regularly. (The negative qualities of pike are not myth material and are rightly ignored by the mythologists.) But, to return to the question in hand: if a 20-lb. pike maintains its quota by swallowing 20 lb. of fish on Monday, Tuesday, and Wednesday, but feels out of sorts on Thursday and gives the whole thing a miss, how does it catch up on Friday? Presumably by eating 40 lb. of fish. A brief calculation will show that if this was the case the record would be broken more often, since for short periods there would be a number of 60-lb. fish about.

Also on the greed legend fringe is the familiar story of the ravenous pike which was the last of its kind in a certain lake, having eaten all the other fish. So ferocious had this pike become that no one would go near the lake for fear the beast would leap out and drag them down. The story invariably ends with the monster pike making a dart at a passing horse and cart, and expiring, gasping, on the bank. When it was measured it was found to be six feet long but was as thin as an eel. This myth ends with the suggestion that had this fish been properly fed with a horse and cart occasionally it would have weighed at least 150 lb. No one ever explains how it kept up all that leaping and snarling about the place if it was as thin as an eel. The poor thing must have been so out of condition that it could hardly have swum at all, and it's an even bet that all its teeth had dropped out long ago.

One more greed sub-myth needs to be mentioned and that concerns the variety of things with which pike have been found choked to death. Here we start at the strictly factual with such animals as voles, moorhens, mallards, etc., and work our way up to the big stuff.

This time the mythologists are concerned largely with cannibalism. To hear two or three pike-lore experts at work is to sit in on a kind of poker game with everybody raising everybody else. And indeed the hands have recognised and relative values. It usually starts with a low opening bet of, 'I once saw a five-pounder choked to death trying to swallow a three-pounder.' (This is about equivalent to a pair of nines.)

'Really, old boy? Now I saw an even more amazing thing. A three-pounder choked to death trying to swallow a five-pounder.' (Two pairs.)

The next man offers 'A nine-pounder with a six-pounder actually inside it.'

The player is raised with: 'Found a ten-pounder, stone dead, choked by *two* four-pounders, one completely swallowed and the other still caught in its throat.' (This rates about the same as a good full-house.)

'A fifteen-pounder with two voles and a mallard drake inside it. Died trying to take my spinner as well.' (Fours at least.)

Does anyone dare raise this, and what might the call be? Ah, yes. Here it comes.

'You won't believe this, old man, but do you know in Ireland I saw a twenty-five pounder with another twenty-five pounder half digested in its stomach.'

You're quite right. We won't believe it. Though we'd like to.

What do I believe myself?

I believe that in my local gravel pit there's a monster of at least 40 lb. that wears a gold ring in its nose bearing an inscription that clearly shows it was given to Henry VIII by Cardinal Wolsey. This fish eats twice its own weight in a day when really on the feed. If it's ever found choked to death, there will be a 140-lb. water bailiff fully dressed in its stomach.

# 12

## *A day on the water*

You have now progressed sufficiently to enjoy a day by, at, or on the water. I give you the choice of prepositions. Your personal selection from these will serve as a fair indication of what sort of angler you already are, or are likely to become.

People who spend the day *by* the water are never going to get much beyond the bent-pin stage. Their whole attitude is expressed by the fact of their by-ness. They are quite content to let the stuff just trickle past while they get on with the sandwiches or maybe even a bad book. True, they may occasionally throw a line into the river but they never really expect anything to happen, and if it does they won't be looking. They'll be lying back zizzing happily with a panama hat tipped soothingly over the eyes. And good luck to them.

*At* the water fishermen are desperately keen, though not necessarily much good at it. Mostly they are in the first throes. They believe that trout and roach spend the whole day with their mouths open just waiting for bait or fly to be plopped at them, whereas, of course, everyone else knows that the sulky beasts feed as daintily and unpredictably as what used to be a deb downing caviare canapés at what used to be a coming-out party. Consequently, *at*-anglers have to be at it all the time, flogging and floating, spinning and spooning, legering and laying-on, but very seldom laying-off. When they're not at the water they're very nearly at their wits' end. This is a diseased state, and, with luck, will pass off like any other febrile condition.

Anglers who talk about being 'on the water' belong to a select group. Mainly they are game fishermen. The word *on* has a splendid superiority about it, and they are well aware of it. Though no one takes very seriously the faint suggestion that they can actually walk supported only by the river's surface, the hint of omnipotence even to a point of levitation remains. The phrase 'Mr (or better still Colonel) So-and-So is on the water' is best delivered by a butler. Whereupon we can all troop out reverently through the french windows just in time

*'The Colonel is on the water, sir'*

to see the immaculate figure of the fisherman pouring himself very dry sherry into a silver cup which he has just taken from his creel while a 4-lb. trout lies shimmering on the grass beside. That is the sort of picture being *on* the water suggests. It's only fair to say that *on*-anglers are very often not as good as *at*-anglers and invariably a lot less contented than *by*-anglers. It depends what you go fishing for.

So now you are going to spend a day (fit in the next word yourself) on, at, or by the water.

Fishermen, being the reticent creatures they are, very rarely speak about what passes during the long silent hours of a day's angling. If you want to find out, you are forced once again to turn to angling literature. In any book you pick up you will come across enthusiastic passages of this sort:

> We'd started out in good heart at crack of dawn on a lovely July day.
>
> By mid-day Charlie's keep-net was bursting while I had twelve good roach to 2½ lb. Then, as the sun blazed down, we suffered that inevitable midday lull, so I decided that I would abandon the float and assault a shoal of enormous chub I had spotted feeding under the willows on my bank. It was the work of an instant to fill a tin with a selection of creeping and crawling things that abounded in the long grass in which we were sitting. Within five minutes I had the first of those chub – he went 5 lb. exactly – flapping on the bank, a victim of the juicy live grasshopper I had dangled in front of his nose.
>
> Charlie meantime had wisely switched to leger tackle, and with the aid of some well-prepared crust was hitting the roach again good and hard,

with an occasional nice bream and even a dace to make for variety.

Then suddenly the fish went off. Oh-ho, I thought to myself, there's Master Esox at work. Flicking out a tiny toothpick float loaded with three dust-shot – I'd quickly made this tackle up – I soon hooked half a dozen live-bait-sized fry. It was the work of a second to pop one of these out on a float paternoster. Ten minutes later the bung went down with a plop and the reel began to scream. No wonder the roach had started to leave Charlie's bait alone. That pike was well and truly hooked so that I had him out in short order. He weighed exactly 6 lb., a nice table fish, so I dispatched him with a smart tap on the skull, whereupon Charlie and I once more came to terms with the red-fins. When we packed up at six o'clock to catch the train home we had filled both our keep-nets. Not an exceptional day, but one I'll always remember with pleasure.

*'Not an exceptional day but one I'll always remember'*

Plainly the author of this piece, and all similar accounts, is a howling liar. What he has done is very similar to modern recording technique. He has taken the best bits from at least twenty sessions and put them together on one long-player. What really happened on the day in question was this . . .

To start with Charlie wasn't up when the writer got to his house. Moreover Charlie, who is a very heavy sleeper, has a wife who dislikes angling and anglers, and the author in particular, if only because he is always arriving at crack of dawn on a fine July morning and pulling the wretched Charlie out of bed. But this fine July morning, when it is already raining like hell, thc alarm hasn't gone off and Charlie is as comatose as a hibernating tench.

So the author wastes an hour and a half under Charlie's bedroom window plaintively imitating a

*Plaintively imitating a cat*

cat since he daren't, because of Charlie's wife, throw a lump of earth at it. Eventually, at a quarter to six, Charlie's head appears at the window and says that as it's raining like hell he doesn't think it's worth going. There follows a brief fraternal exchange. Eventually the pair set off exactly two hours behind schedule, Charlie having forgotten his lunch and his keep-net, largely as a result of the withering fire kept up by Charlie's wife.

Still bickering, they arrive at or by (but definitely not on) the water, having missed one train and waited half an hour for a bus in which Charlie (he would) spilled the live-bait into the conductor's small-change satchel. Every swim for miles is occupied by earlier arrivals, but by midday they are actually fishing in about one foot of water over a revoltingly muddy bottom. The chances of catching anything, let alone a keep-net full of $2\frac{1}{2}$-lb. roach, is about equal to that of seeing a salmon leap Teddington weir next Monday afternoon.

The inevitable midday lull does, in fact, occur, though it is indistinguishable from the inevitable afternoon lull to come and the unavoidable early morning lull they would have experienced had they been there in time.

The author at this point does notice a shoal of something rising under a willow tree, and, though he knows perfectly well that they are bleak, persuades himself, if only to relieve the numbing tedium of Charlie's company, that they are large chub. It is the work of precisely three-quarters of an hour to cajole into a tin one grass-hopper, two nameless and emaciated spiders, and a dispirited woodlouse, which

*He doesn't think it worth going*

is the sum total of creeping or crawling things to be found within four hundred square yards. The author has personally been over every one of these on all fours.

The author then returns to set up the dapping tackle necessary for the premeditated assault on the shoal of chub-bleak and finds to his fury that Charlie has, by one of those unfathomable fishing flukes, actually started to catch some fairish roach. This drives him to such a peak of madness that he empties an entire tin of split-shot into the long grass and puts his foot on the jam sandwich he had been reserving for tea.

At last he creeps up on his belly to the base of the willow tree. Stealthily he opens his bait tin preparatory to impaling one of the creeping and crawling creatures gently on his hook so that he may lower it to the unsuspecting fish. This is exactly what the creeping and crawling creatures have been waiting for. The two spiders immediately creep and crawl out of the tin and run up the angler's sleeve, while the woodlouse has rolled itself into a defensive, unco-operative and totally unassailable brown ball. The grasshopper does exactly what you might have expected it to do: it hops – straight into the middle of the shoal of rising fish.

With savage joy the angler now notices that the fish milling round the stranded grasshopper are in fact bleak, and consequently not worth worrying about. Small consolation, therefore, when a chub of at least 5 lb. ups in the middle of the whole boiling and swallows grasshopper and one small bleak.

Charlie meantime (who has wisely switched to leger tackle) is hauling in not only roach but also bream and occasionally a dace. Moreover, since he left his keep-net behind he's not making it any better by filling up the author's.

In desperation – and not much Oh-ho about it – the author decides that the only thing that can swing the balance back in his favour is to land a fair-sized pike.

Unfortunately he needs live-bait for this and certainly isn't going to ask Charlie. He puts on the tiny toothpick float of the original narrative and then remembers that the dust shot necessary to cock it are somewhere in the long grass. Half an hour later, after sifting several hundredweight of earth through the tail of his cellular vest, he has recovered two BB shot and three more woodlice.

Charlie at this point, while reeling in a small roach, is taken by a 6-lb. pike which clings on in an utterly unnecessary and suicidal fashion until it finds itself on dry land where Charlie heaves it clear of the water with a well-judged flick of the gum-boot.

Readers who took in the first instalments of this simple story will recall how deftly the author dispatched it with a neat blow on top of the skull. The damn thing has landed full toss in his tackle basket so, much as he now hates Charlie, he has to do something about giving it the works. Dazed by all that has happened to him since he left home this morning he seizes the nearest weapon which turns out to be his vacuum flask. A dulcet tinkle of glass reassures him that he has put paid to something at least. There is now nothing at all for tea.

*It is hard to recall exactly who caught what*

Eventually, just as the light is fading, the author catches a gudgeon. It is his only fish of the day.

However, in the pub while they are waiting for the last train, the day seems to lengthen and soften so that the outlines are blurred, and already the low-lights are becoming highlights. It is somewhat hard to recall exactly who caught what and when.

By the time they arrive home they will both be saying that they had a marvellous outing. The strange thing is that they will both believe this.

# 13

## *Minor tactics of the chalk stream*

Fly-fishermen (as a quick reference to my brief *Field Guide to British Anglers* will show) come in two main varieties – wet and dry. The wet sort are a delightfully uncomplicated species. They believe that the proper place for a trout is on a plate with a lump of parsley butter.

Being a dry-fly man is something quite different, and far more difficult. In this branch of the sport one not only has to compete against the fish but against other fishermen. You can learn how to fool the trout in any one of a hundred books called *Dead-low and Gin-Clear*, or some such thing. What I am concerned with here is fooling other dry-fly men.

It must be clearly understood that using a floating imitation of a live insect is a ludicrous way to catch fish, in much the same way that the bullfight is a ridiculous method of exterminating bulls. To begin with, the dry-fly man makes it as hard as he can for himself and everybody else by deliberately choosing to offer the trout a poor facsimile of something they aren't all that interested in anyway. Trout take floating flies rather as human beings eat marrons glacés, and about as often. They'd much rather be rooting around filling their greedy little faces with any old muck they can find floating on or near the bottom.

Second, the last thing the true dry-fly man thinks about is flinging the end-product in a frying pan and doing it up brown.

The recognition of some minute insect at fifty yards' range, the tying of a cunning imitation, the act of casting, the fish rising and possibly even being hooked – these are vital things. After you've got through with that lot, it doesn't much matter if the trout escapes.

From this introduction it may readily be grasped that one can hold one's own as a dry-fly expert without actually catching many fish. No one, luckily, is coming round to weigh your catch at the end of the day, and if you do land a big trout, it's certainly bad form to boast about it, let alone put it in a glass case. There is, therefore, little need to produce the *corpus delicti* to back up your story. We can now go on with the lesson from that point.

Dress plays a large part in establishing the proper dry-fly reputation. There are only two possible alternatives – the perfectionist and the eccentric.

On the whole, the perfectionist is much harder to carry off. If you simply go out and buy the lot and then appear on the water with everything from patent, folding, collapsible landing-net to well-cut fishing jacket, all brand, spanking new, you will run the risk of being written off as filthy rich. After this judgment has been passed you will need to catch a fish at every cast to hold your own.

The correct perfectionist procedure is to buy the best of everything and then let it weather a bit. It may be worth kicking the stuff about for a year or so in the boot cupboard before actually joining a chalk stream syndicate. Even the best-cut Savile Row knickerbockers can be made to look as though they have been around a few seasons once they've been

*Written off as filthy rich*

slept in a couple of times. Thirty-guinea fly-rods easily acquire that five-year-old look after a little light rubbing with sandpaper. An unnecessary repair with sticking plaster helps. Once the shine is off your expensive outfit you can face your fellow members without a qualm.

The eccentric approach is a lot easier, but you must look thoroughly odd. Government surplus gear is not odd enough and can even be held to be *déclassé*. If you are over forty-five years of age, find a very old tweed jacket with a poacher's pocket. The lapels of this coat must be torn to ribbons with the stuffing showing through and looking like aerated cotton-wool. They've got like this, remember, through years of having spare flies stuck into them. On the head, you can't do better than a waterproof deer-stalker which must look as though it has spent at least five years under water, or, better still, under a deer. It should have a hole or two (unexplained) in the crown; a cast coiled round the brim does no harm.

Something really exotic like suède knickerbockers (suitably jagged by barbed wire) and tucked into green lisle stockings will do nicely for below the belt wear, the whole ensemble being bottomed off by shooting gaiters and boots. Finally, never carry a haversack or creel but keep all your impedimenta in rusty cigarette tins disposed about the body.

Young eccentrics can't hope to compete on this level. They must attempt something utterly bizarre, like running shorts, no socks and tennis shoes. On the head they might consider wearing a jungle-green cap or even a surplus bush hat. Abnormality of rod is not so important with the young dry-fly eccentric. After all, he may recently have been given a new one. Older eccentrics should note that they should acquire an ancient split-cane, made by a long dead rod-maker, that is innocent of ferrules and has to be held together with insulating tape; or a greenheart with a set in it like a wishbone.

The essence of being a young eccentric is to give the impression that you dress as you do simply because your outfit is the only possible and practical one if you really want to catch fish. For instance, in shorts (you can explain) you wade far beyond the

*The only possible and practical outfit*

normal limit, provided that you won't mind getting wet of course. Everyone else does mind getting wet, so you score straight away.

Ideally the younger dry-fly man who adopts these tactics should bring in a fish or two occasionally to justify them. All else failing, trout for display purposes can be caught on worms provided a sufficiently early start is made. Otherwise you may have to rely on being thought keen. Keenness is permissible in younger fishermen and earns excellent marks. Note that after thirty-five, keenness is looked upon as rather a bore. You may even be accused of being greedy.

Dress by no means exhausts the gambits available to the dry-fly man. In the main, the others divide themselves into: (a) how to aggrandise your own performance; (b) how to belittle your opponent's. To be effective, and to keep within the traditions of the sport, these exchanges must always be conducted with extreme dead-pan courtesy.

Let us outline some typical dry-fly situations and the correct method of exploiting them.

*Situation One:*

On returning to the fishing hut after eight hours' fruitless flogging you find the Secretary of the Water Committee looking exceptionally pleased with himself. He has obviously had a good day and reveals this by saying diffidently: 'Do any good?'

Whatever you do don't play into his hands with: 'No. Did you?', thus giving him the opportunity to show you three brace of two-pounders.

Try one of these instead:

(a) 'No, but then I *will* keep trying the impossible. I'll have that five-pounder out of the mill race yet. Sat over him all day and only saw him rise once.'

Or (b) 'Oh, trout you mean? No, I've been concentrating on the *chub*. Someone's got to get them out of the water, I suppose.'

Or even (c) 'Funny the way one *develops* as a fly fisherman. A season or two ago I was all for catching a lot of fish. Now I find I'm becoming increasingly interested in simply studying rise forms. Don't know why I bother to take a rod with me.'

Dangerous, this last one, and has to be played with consummate care. You may even have to write a paper on rise forms for the club journal if you consistently go on catching nothing.

*Situation Two:*

You come across a fellow member in the act of netting a nice trout. You obviously cannot deny that he caught it. Unless you are quick, he will exploit you as a witness to his success. You must get in first with one of the following.

(a) 'That *looked* a nice fish. What a pity these trout begin to go back when they get to a pound or so. Takes all the fight out of them.'

(b) 'Good fish that. I say, he looks a bit like one of the hatchery trout they've just put in above us. You can tell these tame fish by their red spots. They soon settle down, of course.'

The beauty of this one is that hatchery fish, as your opponent knows, are extremely unsophisticated when first let loose. They fall for almost anything.

*Very few fly-fishermen cast well when watched by a rival*

Or (c) 'Do you mean to say he fell for a Greenwell as big as that? Well done, old chap!'

The inference of this is that catching the fish at all was a blinding fluke.

*Situation Three:*

The third set of rejoinders and ripostes arises out of what might be called the Challenge Situation. The strategy of attack and evasion here is based on the known fact that very few fly-fishermen are capable of casting well when watched by a rival. Even the genuinely skilful performers select this moment to put their fly into the top of an alder tree or even the lobe of their own left ear. You must therefore be prepared to turn the arrival on the bank of a cynical or hostile watcher to your own advantage.

Here is the set-up. You are surprised in mid-cast to a difficult fish lying close to an overhanging willow on the opposite bank. From here on three things may happen: (1) the most likely is that the fly falls in the tree; (2) the fairly probable is that it drops on the water but is not taken by the fish; (3) the practically impossible is that the trout rises and takes it.

Let us rule out (3) if only for the reason that if you do hook the fish and land it, it will turn out to be a small grayling; (2) is depressing, because you will, after having got the thing down safely on the water, have to cast again.

The tree position (1) may look entirely hopeless. Not so, however. Simply turn to your companion, who will now be standing with punctilious respect for your endeavours as if waiting for you to drive off from the first tee at St Andrews, and say: 'Been trying to drop a fly on those leaves for hours. Now if I can only persuade it to slide off naturally I do believe he'll fall for it.'

Only you know that the point of the hook is buried above the barb in the bark of the tree and that the cast is tied three times round a branch. When you do at last mutter: 'Dammit, got caught up, I'm afraid', your opponent can only answer 'Bad luck', and move on.

If you are not actually casting when your opponent appears, and if he shows signs of hanging round, simply say to him: 'That big chap under the tree over there beats me hollow. Here, you have a throw at him.' Only the very callow will actually try.

Or you can, if you spot your opponent coming soon enough, start to change a fly. The danger here is that he will stop to chat to you, and that the fish may rise during this time. If it does so and he remarks on it, come back casually with: 'Oh, that one? Had him on twice. Ruddy great chub.'

A few notes concerning attack and defence when staying at fishing hotels may be useful. All that I have said regarding dress applies, only more so. If a perfectionist, always try to arrive at a meal-time and unload your gear, apparently endlessly, from the boot of the car in view of as many guests as possible.

Eccentrics might try driving up with their rod already assembled and sticking out of the car's back window. Having signed the hotel register they should leave immediately, and as obviously as possible, to view the water. Binoculars and polarised spectacles must be in evidence.

Whatever your style of fishing, be seen as soon as possible in some prominent place, like the bar, tying your own flies. Even if you have had to take lessons specially for the trip, it will be worth it.

If you catch a really good fish on your first day, be careful to come in late. Blunder into the bar carrying your catch casually in a landing net and say in a slightly embarrassed fashion: 'Can anybody tell me to whom one gives these things?'

Lack of success can be countered with throw-away dialogue that combines a suggestion of great technical knowledge with charming and natural modesty. Thus: 'Of course, I don't claim to be much of a fisherman but I really think they should do something about putting down fly-boards.' (Or cutting the weed, or restocking: any of these will do.)

Finally a great deal can be achieved through clever use of the hotel game book or fishing diary. You can not only get the measure of your opponents from this but you can also score a point or two yourself.

Let us take a specimen example. Among the previous day's entries you note the following:

| FISH | TAKEN ON | CONDITIONS | REMARKS | NAME |
|---|---|---|---|---|
| *trout* 11 *oz.*<br>10½ *oz.*<br>12 *oz.*<br>(*doubt-*<br>*ful*)<br>11 *oz.*<br>11 *oz.*<br>14 *oz.* | *My usual hackled Wickham* | *Blustery S.E. wind Light bright* | *Seemed to be coming short* | *Colonel Ponsonby-Lavers* |

Below this you write your own entry.

| | | | | |
|---|---|---|---|---|
| *trout* 1 *lb.* 4 *oz.* | *Size* 00 *Tup tied with Gantron body* | *Perfect* | *Should have had two more about the same size* | *C. Willock* |

A brief analysis shows that you have scored at least three direct hits, and you have left it very hard for anyone coming after you to go one better.

The weight limit for the hotel water is 12 oz. What, then, was the Colonel doing boasting about all those immature troutlings? That '12 oz. (doubtful)' entry was a lamentable attempt to impress with honesty. His assumption, too, that everybody knows he is a one-fly man will do him little good in the eyes of his fellow guests, not, at least, until he has better results to show. 'Blustery S.E. wind', etc., though patently a true picture of the conditions, is too obviously an alibi, as is 'seemed to be coming short'. If they were, then how did he hook all that undersized stuff? After this lot, even the signature is not entirely free from suspicion.

Now take your own. One decent fish and to heck with the tiddlers. You used a very small fly (always worth a point or two) and obviously tied it yourself with an experimental body (someone is bound to ask you later what Gantron is when you can further entrench yourself with a short fly-tying demonstration). No excuses, please note, about the weather. The word 'perfect' will be doubly effective because everyone else thought – and quite rightly so – that conditions were thoroughly foul. Lastly, that nice touch of modesty – 'should have had two more'.

The only trouble is that you've started too well.

Perhaps, after this, the best thing is to leave the hotel next day.

*'Can anybody tell me to whom one gives these things?'*

# 14

## *A layman's guide to anglers*

A world that has mastered nuclear physics and the basic steps in space travel should be able to understand anglers. So far every attempt to do so has been a dismal wash-out.

The best the lay public can manage is to stick little decorated notices up in fishing hotels bearing imbecile rhymes about the angler returning at close of day smelling of strong drink and having no truth in him.

That doddering pedant Dr Johnson (as reported by Colonel Peter Hawker) was partly responsible for this irresponsible attitude with his often-quoted worm-on-one-end-and-fool-on-the-other line. Since when other red-nosed comedians have assumed that anglers are essentially comical.

I shall close this short work, therefore, with a brief layman's guide to angler handling, rather in the manner that during the last war the U.S. Forces issued invading G.I.'s with a booklet of local manners and mores so that their reception by the natives might be tolerably friendly. (Example: Don't ask for ice water at the Ritz: they may not have a fridge, and it will only embarrass the *maître d'hôtel, pron. Maytrer doughtel.*)

First, then, you must realise that anglers are just people like you. The fact that they like to sit by rivers instead of shouting their stupid heads off at football matches is strange, perhaps, but no more so than, say, the fact that some Indians wear loincloths without other Indians minding.

It may seem absurd to you that anglers are content to sit in one place in a biting east wind all day watching a float. On the other hand, it probably strikes them as odd that you prefer to go blind with your eyeballs stuck to the telly.

Try to repress any astonishment you may feel when anglers tell you that they put (please note 'put', not 'throw') back many of the fish they catch. I quite agree that this is, on the face of it, ridiculous, but the simple-hearted and often confused chaps are sensitive on this point.

As an angler once remarked to a gardening friend of mine who was having a good manury, potting-shed laugh at this throwing 'em back business: 'And I suppose when your tulips have flowered you pull up the ruddy things and chuck them in the incinerator.'

The point he was, I think, trying to make, however inadequately, was that having given the gardener his fun the tulips, if stuck back in the earth at the right time, would let him have another run for his money. The same, it seems, goes for fish. Once in the dustbin or inside a dirty great black cat their sporting quality is very largely lost to others. Naturally, if the angler wants to eat his fish that's his business, but very little of what he catches is edible.

Make a point of avoiding such remarks as: 'What do you do all day when you're sitting there watching that float thing?' Or, 'I suppose fishing gives you plenty of time to think.'

*Very little of what the angler catches is edible*

Angling is a harmless form of monomania. That study in still-life squatting on the canal bank is utterly and totally absorbed by the thought that at the very next millionth of a second his float is going to dart under to the pull of the fish of a lifetime.

So obsessed is he by this fantasy that his brain feels as if it is anchored through the eye-sockets to the very tip of that float. He is not thinking of the row he had with his wife about the kippers being burnt, or what he's going to tell that shop steward on Monday. He is thinking, lunatic as it may appear, exclusively about catching fish.

By the same token it is tactless to say to a fisherman: 'I wish I had your patience.' This is about the equivalent of remarking to a gorilla: 'I wish I had your ear for music.'

Both will look at you with a blank stare. Either may strike you. And for the same reasons. Neither knows what the hell you're talking about, and each has a vague idea that you're being insulting.

Fishermen may be many things, but they are not patient. They are probably the most impatient men on earth. They are not just sitting there waiting for something to happen. They are expecting, even willing, something to happen, now, the very next second, or the second after that. Even when it doesn't happen, they still can't believe that it won't, but they know that the very instant they stop being prepared for it to happen, it will. That is why they are impatient.

It is a common lay belief that all fishermen are liars, and that the index of their falsehoods is the distance between their outstretched arms.

Fishermen are no more liars than golfers and, as is well known, the honest handicap player is always precise as to the number of putts he took, at least when recounting his experiences to his friends in the bar. Moreover if a fisherman *was* disposed to lie, he'd do it in avoirdupois rather than linear measure. Fish, the layman should note, are measured in poundage not feet, if only because many of them, quite frankly, don't extend much beyond inches.

Nor should the well-wisher make the elementary mistake of commiserating with or congratulating the angler upon the state of the weather with such bromides as: 'I suppose you don't mind the rain because it makes them bite', or 'a bit bright for fishing, isn't it?'

You'll get no thanks for it, whatever you say.

Despite a number of meteorological superstitions like 'wind in the south blows the bait into the fish's mouth', anglers know that there is no sort of weather that is good, let alone ideal, for fishing. So give up. Some days are better than others, but that's as far as any sensible fisherman will go. Damn it, in a business that has so many variables and imponderables, anglers have to hold tight to one steady source of alibi material. And everybody, even non-anglers, can understand that the weather is to blame for almost everything.

A word, too, on angler-watching.

Anglers don't mind you watching. In fact they rather like it. Except when you lean over their shoulder, play rounders on the bank with your yelping offspring, throw sticks for a large black

*Anglers don't mind you watching*

Labrador, produce a portable radio, sail round in circles just short of their floats in a cabin cruiser, feed swans, dance about in a white shirt, ask if your son can look at their tackle, pick up the fish in their keep-nets, trip over their landing-net handles, let your dog eat their ground bait, tell them that you used to catch marlin in Florida, or say that you can't see anything in fishing yourself.

And particularly this last one, for, if you can't see anything in it yourself, what the hell are you doing standing there gawping on the off-chance that you'll catch a glimpse of a fish actually being caught? Or are you just trying to annoy?

Furthermore, if you're one of those people who goes around saying: 'I've watched for hours and do you know I've never seen them catch anything worth having,' just reflect on this.

Did you *really* watch for hours?

In a good day, a really good day, a fisherman might catch half a dozen fish worth talking about. A fishing day can be reckoned as lasting at least six hours. That seems to make the rate of striking about every hour on the hour. What is more—the very fact that you were there wearing a white shirt, with your odious offspring, black Labrador, portable radio, cabin cruiser, herd of swans, picking up keep-nets, tripping over gear, feeding your mongrel on other people's gentles, and expressing your opinion on the futility of the whole undertaking, quite probably put the fish off.

But take heart, if you think you have offended, you haven't even really begun. After all you could have said: *'Had any luck yet?'*

For anglers, bless them, believe that luck doesn't enter into it. Catching fish, the poor idiots insist, is entirely a matter of skill.

*'Had any luck yet?'*

# *Glossary*

*Some useful terms used in this book and elsewhere explained for non-anglers.*

| | |
|---|---|
| Bleak | outlook at 3 p.m. on a blank day. |
| Bloodworms | euphemism for recalcitrant bait. |
| Bullhead | useful epithet. |
| Bull, trout | any other member's fishing story. |
| Bung | well-known angling toast. |
| Char | and very refreshing too. |
| Creeper | member trying to get round the secretary. |
| Drag | short puff between casts. |
| Dun | third reminder that subscription is due. |
| Floater | cheque returned by the secretary. |
| Fly-rod | one who knows it all. |
| Jack | familiar name for other anglers. |
| Lunn's particular | and quite right, too. |
| Luce | but only her friends call her this. |
| Mallard and Claret | those days are gone, alas. |

| | |
|---|---|
| Mayfly | insect, remarkable for being seen only in June. |
| Pick-up | one thing at a time please. We're fishing now. |
| Pouting | female expression to greet returning angler. |
| Pollan | fatal to hay fever sufferers. |
| Priest | seen on almost any water, especially in Ireland. |
| Salmo ferox | irate game fishermen. |
| Sheffield basket | local term of abuse. |
| Sink-and-draw | to order another round. |
| Wickham's Fancy | but don't let him hear you say so. |